Crochet HATS

pil

Publications International, Ltd.

Consulting by Heidi Beazley and Zee Wang
Patterns by Zee Wang

Written by Beth Taylor

Photo styling by Ewelina Rusek and Amy Stark

Photography by Christopher Hiltz
Additional photography from Getty and Shutterstock.com

Crochet symbols and abbreviations from Craft Yarn Council's www.YarnStandards.com

Louis Weber, CEO
Publications International, Ltd.
8140 Lehigh Avenue
Morton Grove, IL 60053

ISBN: 978-1-63938-786-1

Manufactured in China.

8 7 6 5 4 3 2 1

Contents

GETTING STARTED

HAT PATTERNS

Started

What You'll Need

CROCHET HOOKS

Crochet hooks can be made from aluminum, plastic, wood, or bamboo. They are available in a wide range of sizes and are used with an assortment of yarns. Steel hooks are the smallest and are often used with fine thread in delicate crochet work, such as lace and doilies. Most patterns and yarn labels recommend a hook size. Select a crochet hook that feels comfortable to you and works well with your project and yarn.

COMMON HOOK SIZES

Metric size	U.S. size
2.25 mm	B-1
2.5 mm	
2.75 mm	C-2
3.125 mm	D
3.25 mm	D-3
3.5 mm	E-4
3.75 mm	F-5
4 mm	G-6
4.25 mm	G
4.5 mm	7
5 mm	H-8
5.25 mm	I
5.5 mm	I-9
5.75 mm	J
6 mm	J-10
6.5 mm	K-10.5
7 mm	
8 mm	L-11
9 mm	M/N-13
10 mm	N/P-15
11.5 mm	P-16
12 mm	
15 mm	P/Q
15.75 mm	Q
16 mm	Q
19 mm	S
25 mm	T/U/X
30 mm	T/X

What You'll Need

NEEDLES

Tapestry or yarn needles have a blunt tip and an eye large enough to accommodate thick yarns. These special needles can be used to weave in yarn tails or sew crocheted pieces together.

STITCH MARKERS

As their name suggests, stitch markers are designed to mark your stitches. They can be used to mark a certain number of stitches, the beginning of a round, or where to make a particular stitch. Stitch markers must have openings so that they can be easily removed. You can purchase stitch markers, or improvise with pins, earrings, or safety pins.

PINS

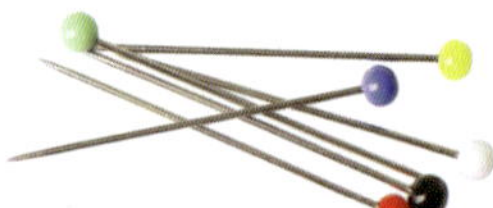

Use long, rustproof pins for blocking and pinning seams together. Pins can also serve as stitch markers. Select pins with large, colorful heads that won't get lost in your crochet work.

MEASUREMENT TOOLS

A tailor's tape measure is a must-have tool when taking body and head measurements, which is especially important before making garments or hats. You can use a tape measure or a ruler to measure gauge.

HAT SIZING

For an accurate head circumference measure, place a tape measure across the middle of the forehead and wrap all the way around the head. Make sure the tape measure is straight (not twisted) and snug. Hat length is measured from the top at the crown down to the bottom edge or brim.

	Circumference (in)	Circumference (cm)
Preemie	9–12"	23–30.5 cm
Baby	14–16"	35.5–40.5 cm
Toddler	16–18"	40.5–46 cm
Child	18–20"	46–51 cm
Tween	20–22"	51–56 cm
Adult woman	21–23"	53–58.5 cm
Adult man	22–24"	56–61 cm

All About Yarn

YARN FOR BEGINNERS

Before starting any new crochet project, you must select your yarn. For beginners learning the basic stitches, select a simple cotton yarn that is light colored, smooth, and sturdy. It's harder to see your stitches with dark colored yarn. Avoid fuzzy and loosely woven yarns that fray easily.

YARN FIBERS

Natural fibers

Cotton, linen, and hemp yarns are made from plant fibers. They are lightweight, breathable, and machine washable. Mercerized cotton has undergone a chemical process that results in stronger, shinier yarn.

Yarns made from animal fibers include wool, silk, cashmere, mohair, alpaca, and angora. These animal fibers are much warmer than plant fibers. Both types of natural fibers offer a bit of stretch.

Synthetic fibers

Yarns made from synthetic fibers include nylon, rayon, acrylic, and polyester. Synthetic yarns are usually less expensive than natural fibers, but are less breathable and pill more easily.

Novelty and specialty yarns

Novelty and specialty yarns can be tricky to work with, but create a distinctive look. They include bouclé, ladder, eyelash, and chenille. While great for trims and accessories, novelty yarn is not best for beginners.

SELECTING YOUR YARN

Each package of store-bought yarn has a label listing the yarn's length, fiber content, and weight. Yarn weight refers to the thickness of a yarn. It ranges from the thinnest embroidery thread to the bulkiest yarn. Yarn labels also recommend hook size—just look for the crochet hook symbol to find the U.S. and metric hook size.

Yarn Weight Guidelines

Yarn types: Fingering, lace, and 10-count crochet thread
Recommended hook sizes (metric): 1.5–2.25 mm
Recommended hook sizes (U.S.): Steel 6 to B-1
Crochet gauge range: 32–42 double crochet stitches to 4 in.

Yarn types: Sock, fingering, and baby
Recommended hook sizes (metric): 2.25–3.5 mm
Recommended hook sizes (U.S.): B-1 to E-4
Crochet gauge range: 21–32 single crochet stitches to 4 in.

Yarn types: Sport and baby
Recommended hook sizes (metric): 3.5–4.5 mm
Recommended hook sizes (U.S.): E-4 to 7
Crochet gauge range: 16–20 single crochet stitches to 4 in.

Yarn types: Double knitting and light worsted
Recommended hook sizes (metric): 4.5–5.5 mm
Recommended hook sizes (U.S.): 7 to I-9
Crochet gauge range: 12–17 single crochet stitches to 4 in.

Yarn types: Afghan, aran, and worsted
Recommended hook sizes (metric): 5.5–6.5 mm
Recommended hook sizes (U.S.): I-9 to K-10.5
Crochet gauge range: 11–14 single crochet stitches to 4 in.

Yarn types: Chunky, craft, and rug
Recommended hook sizes (metric): 6.5–9 mm
Recommended hook sizes (U.S.): K-10.5 to M/N-13
Crochet gauge range: 8–11 single crochet stitches to 4 in.

Yarn types: Bulky and roving
Recommended hook sizes (metric): 9–15 mm
Recommended hook sizes (U.S.): M/N-13 to P/Q
Crochet gauge range: 7–9 single crochet stitches to 4 in.

Yarn types: Jumbo and roving
Recommended hook sizes (metric): 15 mm and larger
Recommended hook sizes (U.S.): P/Q and larger
Crochet gauge range: 6 single crochet stitches and fewer to 4 in.

Source: Craft Yarn Council's www.YarnStandards.com

Holding the Hook

Pencil Hold

Knife Hold

Tip: The instructions and photographs in this book are intended for right-handed crocheters. If you are a lefty, try holding up a mirror to the edge of a photograph to see the left-handed version.

Holding the Yarn

1

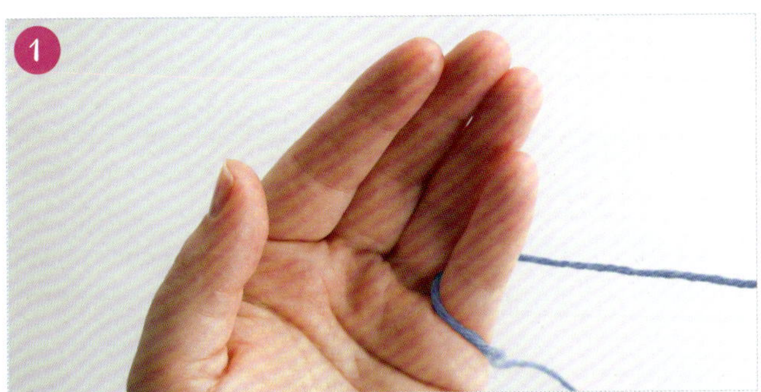

With your palm facing up, weave the working yarn (the yarn coming from the ball) between your pinky and ring fingers. Wrap the yarn clockwise around your pinky.

2

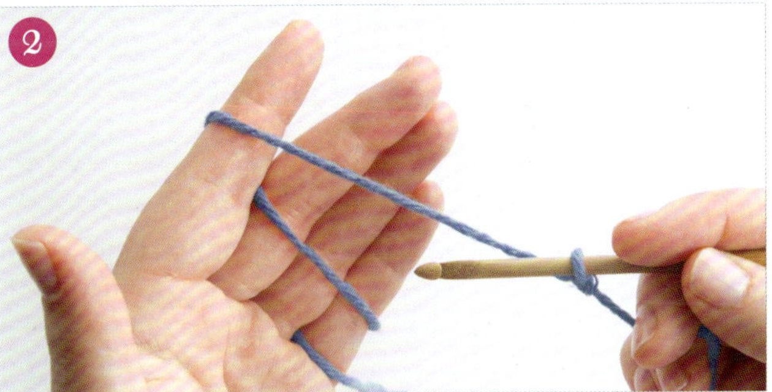

Take the yarn across your ring and middle fingers. Then wrap the yarn under and around your index finger.

3

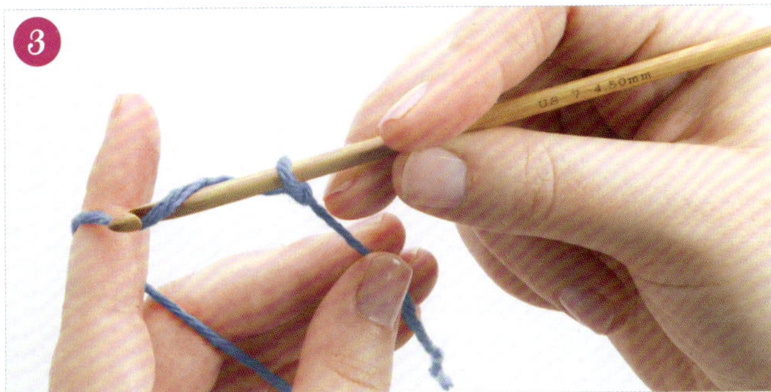

Hold the yarn under the slip knot with your left thumb and middle finger.

Tip: There are many ways to hold your yarn. Experiment with different methods until you find what is most comfortable for you.

Making a Slip Knot

**The first step in most crochet projects is a slip knot.
The slip knot is what attaches the yarn to your hook.**

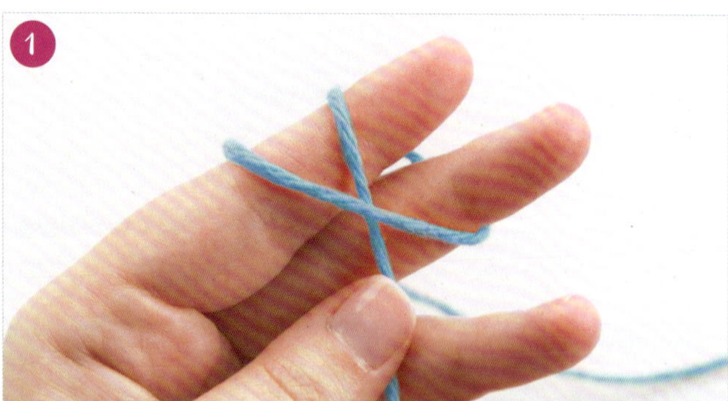

Wrap the yarn around your index and middle fingers on your yarn hand to create an X.

From the top, insert your hook under the first loop to grab the second loop.

Draw the second loop you just grabbed under and up through the first loop.

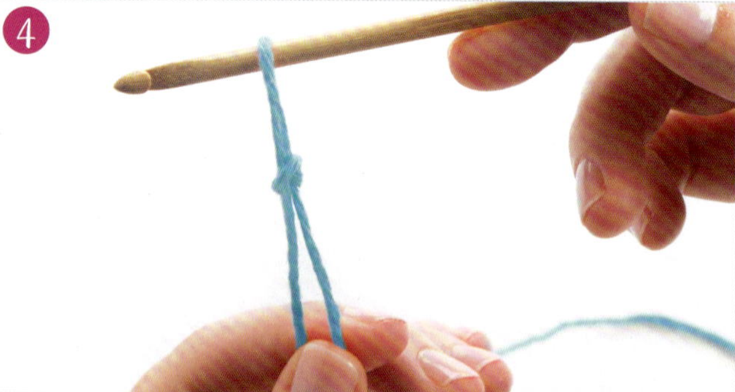

Slide your fingers out. Pull your hook up while gently pulling both ends of the yarn down.

Pull the ends of the yarn to tighten the slip knot close to your hook.

With a finished slip knot around your hook, you are ready to start crocheting.

Chain Stitch (CH)

Crochet often begins with a series of chain stitches used to make up the first row. This is called the foundation chain and is the basic start to most crochet projects.

Start with a slip knot on your hook. Hold the yarn tail for tension.

Bring the working yarn (the yarn coming from the ball) over your hook from back to front. This is called yarn over (yo).

Draw this section of yarn back through the slip knot. You will have 1 new loop on your hook when your first chain stitch is complete.

Yarn over again.

Draw this section of yarn through the loop on your hook. You will have 1 new loop on your hook each time you complete a chain stitch.

Repeat steps 4–5 until your foundation chain has the required number of chain stitches.

Counting Chains

Crochet patterns usually begin by telling you the number of chains needed for the foundation chain.

IDENTIFYING THE FRONT AND BACK

The front of the foundation chain looks like a braid with a series of Vs. The back side of the foundation chain has a vertical ridge of bumps running down the middle from your hook to the end of the chain. Count chains from the front side.

COUNTING

Begin counting from the top of the foundation chain. Do not count the loop on your hook or the slip knot on the bottom. Count only completed, V-shaped chain stitches. This example has 13 completed chain stitches.

Tip: When creating a long foundation chain, it is helpful to use stitch markers every 10 or 20 stitches to make counting easier.

Turning Chains (TCH)

Stitch	Number of Turning Chains
Slip stitch	0
Single crochet	1
Half double crochet	2
Double crochet	3
Treble crochet	4

Each crochet stitch requires a specific number of turning chains at the beginning or end of a row. The number of extra stitches needed for the turning chain is added to the number needed for the foundation chain.

Tension

Tension keeps your stitches neat and consistent. Make sure the chains in your foundation chain are even and loose enough to allow your hook back into those chains for the next row.

Too loose

Too tight

Just right

Slip Stitch (SL ST)

The slip stitch is one of the most basic crochet stitches and is often used for joining.

1 Start with a foundation chain on your hook. Insert your hook from front to back into the second chain from your hook. There are 2 loops on your hook.

2 Yarn over, bringing the working yarn over your hook from back to front.

3 Draw the yarn through both loops on your hook. You will have 1 new loop on your hook when your first slip stitch is complete.

Single Crochet (SC)

HOW TO SINGLE CROCHET:

To begin a row of single crochet, first stitch a foundation chain to the desired length. Add 1 extra chain stitch for the turning chain.

Insert your hook from front to back into the second chain stitch from your hook. There will now be 2 loops on your hook.

Yarn over. Draw this yarn through the first loop on your hook. There will be 2 loops on your hook.

Yarn over again and draw this yarn through both loops on your hook. You will have 1 loop remaining on your hook when your first single crochet is complete.

Insert your hook into the next chain stitch. Repeat steps 2–3 to complete another single crochet stitch.

Repeat step 4, working a single crochet stitch into each chain. At the end of the row, make 1 chain stitch for the turning chain.

Turn your work so that the opposite side faces you. Insert your hook into the first single crochet stitch of the previous row and repeat steps 2–3. (Skip the turning chain.)

Insert your hook into the next stitch and repeat steps 2–3, working a single crochet stitch into each single crochet of the previous row.

Repeat step 7 to continue the pattern. At the end of this and all subsequent rows, chain 1 for the turning chain and turn your work.

Half Double Crochet (HDC)

HOW TO HALF DOUBLE CROCHET:

To begin a row of half double crochet, first stitch a foundation chain to the desired length. Add 2 extra chain stitches for the turning chain.

Yarn over. With this yarn over, insert your hook into the third chain stitch from your hook. There will be 3 loops on your hook.

Yarn over again. Draw this yarn through the first loop only. There will still be 3 loops on your hook.

Yarn over and draw this yarn through all 3 loops on your hook.

You will have 1 loop on your hook when your first half double crochet is complete.

Yarn over. With this yarn over, insert your hook into the next chain stitch. There will be 3 loops on your hook. Repeat steps 2–4 to complete another half double crochet stitch.

Repeat step 5, working a half double crochet stitch into each chain stitch. At the end of the row, chain 2 for the turning chain.

Turn your work so that the opposite side faces you. Yarn over and insert your hook into the second stitch. (The turning chain counts as the first half double crochet stitch in this row.) Repeat steps 2–4 to complete the half double crochet stitch.

Repeat step 5 to continue making half double crochet stitches into each stitch of the previous row. At the end of this and all subsequent rows, chain 2 for the turning chain and turn.

Double Crochet (DC)

HOW TO DOUBLE CROCHET:

To begin a row of double crochet, first stitch a foundation chain to the desired length. Add 3 extra chain stitches for the turning chain.

Yarn over. With this yarn over, insert your hook into the fourth chain stitch from your hook. There will be 3 loops on your hook.

Yarn over. Draw this yarn through the first loop on your hook. There will be 3 loops on your hook.

Yarn over. Draw this yarn through the first 2 loops on your hook only. There will now be 2 loops on your hook.

Yarn over again. Draw this yarn through the remaining 2 loops on your hook. You will have 1 loop on your hook when your first double crochet is complete.

Yarn over. Insert your hook into the next chain stitch. Repeat steps 2–4 to complete another double crochet stitch.

Repeat step 5, working a double crochet stitch into each chain stitch. At the end of the row, chain 3 for the turning chain. Turn your work so that the opposite side faces you.

Yarn over and insert your hook into the second stitch. (The turning chain counts as the first double crochet stitch in this row.) Repeat steps 2–4 to complete the double crochet stitch.

Repeat step 5 to continue making double crochet stitches into each stitch of the previous row. At the end of this and all subsequent rows, chain 3 for the turning chain and turn.

Treble Crochet (TR)

HOW TO TREBLE CROCHET:

To begin a row of treble crochet, first stitch a foundation chain to the desired length. Add 4 extra chain stitches for the turning chain.

Yarn over twice. Insert your hook into the fifth chain stitch from your hook. There will now be 4 loops on your hook.

Yarn over once. Draw this yarn through the first loop on your hook. There will be 4 loops on your hook.

Yarn over once. Draw this yarn through the first 2 loops on your hook. There will be 3 loops on your hook.

Yarn over once. Draw this yarn through the first 2 loops on your hook again. There will be 2 loops on your hook.

Yarn over once. Draw the yarn through the remaining 2 loops on your hook. You will have 1 loop on your hook when your first treble crochet is complete.

Yarn over twice and insert your hook into the next chain stitch. Repeat steps 2–5 to complete another treble crochet stitch.

Repeat step 6, working a treble crochet stitch into each chain. At the end of the row, chain 4 for the turning chain. Turn your work so that the opposite side faces you. Yarn over twice and insert your hook into the second stitch. Repeat steps 2–5 to complete the treble crochet stitch.

Repeat step 6 to continue making treble crochet stitches into each stitch of the previous row. At the end of this and all subsequent rows, chain 4 for the turning chain and turn.

Decreasing Stitches (DEC)

To decrease within a row or round, combine multiple stitches together.

SINGLE CROCHET 2 TOGETHER (sc2tog)

Insert your hook into the next stitch as you would to start a single crochet.

Yarn over and draw this yarn through the stitch. There are now 2 loops on your hook.

Insert your hook into the next stitch. Yarn over and draw this yarn through the stitch. There are 3 loops on your hook.

Yarn over and draw this yarn through all 3 loops on your hook. You will have 1 loop on your hook when your first single crochet 2 together (sc2tog) is complete.

DOUBLE CROCHET 2 TOGETHER (dc2tog)

Yarn over and insert hook into next stitch. Yarn over and draw yarn through stitch. Yarn over and draw yarn through first 2 loops. You will have 2 loops on hook.

Yarn over and insert hook into next stitch. Yarn over and draw yarn through stitch. Yarn over and draw yarn through first 2 loops. You will have 3 loops on hook.

Yarn over and draw this yarn through all 3 loops on your hook. You will have 1 loop on your hook when your first double crochet 2 together (dc2tog) is complete.

Increasing Stitches (INC)

To increase within a row or round, work multiple stitches into the same stitch.

SINGLE CROCHET INCREASE (sc inc)

Insert your hook back into the same stitch you did your last single crochet in. Work another single crochet into that same stitch.

You will have 1 loop on your hook when your first single crochet increase is complete.

DOUBLE CROCHET INCREASE (dc inc)

Insert your hook back into the same stitch in the previous row. Work another double crochet into that same stitch.

You will have 1 loop on your hook when your first double crochet increase is complete.

Puffs

Puffs are textured stitches.

To make puffs using half double crochet, start with a foundation chain that has any odd number of chains.

How to half double crochet 4 together (hdc4tog):

1. Yarn over and insert your hook into the chain space.
2. Yarn over and draw the loop through. You will have 3 loops on your hook. It's important to keep your loops taller so it's easier to draw through them at the end.
3. Repeat steps 1-2 two more times until you have 7 loops on your hook. (With every repeat, you add 2 more loops to your hook.)
4. Yarn over and draw through all 7 loops. There will be 1 loop left on your hook.

ROW 1:

1

In the second chain from your hook, work 1 single crochet stitch.

2

Chain 1. Skip 1 chain and work 1 single crochet into the next chain. Repeat step 2 across the row.

3 At the end of the row, chain 2 for the turning chain and turn your work so that the opposite side faces you.

ROW 2:

1. Skip the first stitch. The turning chain counts as the first half double crochet in this row.

In the next chain space, work 4 half double crochet stitches together (hdc4tog) following the tip instructions, until you have 7 loops on your hook.

Yarn over and draw through all 7 loops on your hook. There will be 1 loop left when your 4 half double crochets are complete.

Chain 1 to secure and complete the puff.

Repeat steps 2–4 across the row, ending with 1 half double crochet in the last stitch of the previous row.

Chain 1 for the turning chain and turn your work so the opposite side faces you.

ROW 3:

1. Work 1 single crochet into the first stitch.
2. Chain 1. Skip 1 chain and work 1 single crochet into the next stitch.
3. Repeat step 2 across the row.

Repeat rows 2–3 to continue the pattern.

Basketweave

This basketweave uses alternating front post double crochet (FPdc) and back post double crochet (BPdc) stitches. Post stitches are sometimes called raised stitches.

Start with a foundation chain that has a multiple of 6 chains, plus 4.

FRONT & BACK POSTS

Instead of inserting your hook into a stitch or space, you insert it around the front or back of a post. The stitches are worked the same as usual. The only difference is where your hook is inserted.

FRONT POSTS

Insert your hook under the post from the front side.

BACK POSTS

Insert your hook under the post from the back side.

ROW 1:

In the 4th chain from your hook, work 1 double crochet. Continue across the row, working 1 double crochet into each chain.

Chain 2 for the turning chain and turn your work so that the opposite side faces you.

ROW 2:

Work 1 double crochet around the 2nd front post of the previous row (FPdc). To do this, yarn over (because you are doing a double crochet) and insert your hook, from the front, under the 2nd post. Finish your double crochet as usual.

Work a FPdc stitch around the next 2 posts so there are a total of 3.

Work 1 double crochet around the next back post (BPdc). To do this, yarn over (because you are doing a double crochet) and insert your hook, from the back side, under the next post. Finish your double crochet as usual.

Work a BPdc stitch around the next 2 posts so there are a total of 3.

Continue across the row, alternating 3 FPdc stitches with 3 BPdc stitches. Finish the row by working 1 double crochet into the top chain of the turning chain.

Chain 2 for the turning chain and turn your work so that the opposite side faces you.

ROW 3:

1. Repeat row 2, alternating 3 FPdc stitches with 3 BPdc stitches across the row. Work 1 double crochet into the top of the turning chain. Chain 2 and turn.

ROW 4:

1. Work 1 BPdc stitch around the 2nd post. Work 1 BPdc stitch around the next 2 posts for a total of 3 BPdc stitches.

2. Work 1 FPdc stitch around the next 3 posts for a total of 3 FPdc stitches. Continue across the row, alternating 3 BPdc stitches with 3 FPdc stitches.

3. Work 1 double crochet into the top of the last turning chain.

4. Chain 2 for the turning chain and turn your work so that the opposite side faces you.

ROW 5:

1. Repeat row 4, alternating 3 BPdc stitches with 3 FPdc stitches across the row. Work 1 double crochet into the top of the turning chain. Chain 2 and turn.

Repeat rows 2–5 to continue the pattern.

Front & Back Loops (FL & BL)

Working into the front or back loop only will create a unique texture and line. These examples use half double crochet, but you can use these techniques with other stitches.

Tip: When your crochet work is in front of you, the front loop is the loop closer to you, while the back loop is farther from you.

FRONT LOOPS

To work a half double crochet stitch into the front loop only (or flo), yarn over and insert your hook into only the front loop closer to you. Complete the stitch as usual.

Continue working half double crochet stitches into only the front loops of the stitches in the previous row or round until you reach the end of the row/round. This creates a line.

BACK LOOPS

To work a half double crochet stitch into the back loop only (or blo), yarn over and insert your hook into only the back loop farther from you. Complete the stitch as usual.

Continue working half double crochet stitches into only the back loops of the stitches in the previous row or round until you reach the end. This creates another line.

Working into Spaces

Some patterns will ask you to work into a space rather than a stitch of a previous row or round. This technique is demonstrated below using double crochet, but you can use other stitches.

Start at the position where you want to work into a space. Yarn over.

Insert your hook from front to back into the space (instead of the stitch). Yarn over and draw this yarn through the space.

Finish your double crochet as usual. You will have 1 loop on your hook when your first double crochet stitch into the space is complete.

Here is the row finished with double crochet stitches worked into the spaces.

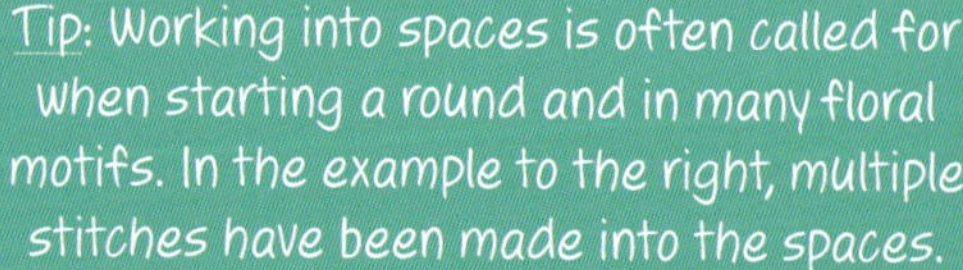

Tip: Working into spaces is often called for when starting a round and in many floral motifs. In the example to the right, multiple stitches have been made into the spaces.

Working in Rounds

To begin working in rounds, you have to first start with a center ring. There are 2 different methods for starting a round: with a chain stitch ring or a magic circle.

CHAIN STITCH RING

The chain stitch ring is made up of chain stitches that are joined together to form a ring. This method leaves a small opening in the center of your round.

Tip: Patterns will tell you how many chains to start with and what stitches to use. This example uses single crochet.

1. Chain 5 for a foundation chain. Insert your hook back into the first chain you made.

2. Work a slip stitch into that chain to form a ring.

3. Insert your hook into the center of the ring. Work a single crochet stitch into the ring.

4. Continue working single crochet stitches into the ring until you have made the required number of stitches. (For this example, 6 single crochet stitches.)

Work a slip stitch into the first single crochet you made to close up the ring.

You are now ready to start a round.
(See page 34.)

MAGIC CIRCLE

The magic circle forms a ring with your yarn to which your first round of stitches are attached. The ends are pulled to leave no opening in the center. That's the magic!

> Tip: A chain stitch ring can replace a magic circle in a pattern.

Loop the yarn around your fingers as shown to form an X.

Take your hook under the bottom strand of the X. Use your hook to draw the other strand under the bottom strand. It will form a loose loop on your hook.

Remove the circle of yarn from your fingers. Yarn over. Draw this yarn through the loop on your hook. (This does not count as your first single crochet stitch.)

With your magic circle complete, you should now have a circle with the tail and the working yarn on the left side.

Insert your hook into the center of the circle. You are going to work a single crochet into that space. Yarn over and draw this yarn through the circle and tail. You will have 2 loops on your hook.

Yarn over again and draw this yarn through the remaining 2 loops on your hook. You will have 1 loop on your hook when your first single crochet stitch into the circle is complete.

Continue working the required number of single crochet stitches into the circle, making sure you are always working around the circle and the tail. If you run out of tail, pull it slightly. This closes the circle a little, but allows you to have a longer tail to work around.

When you have worked 6 single crochet stitches into the circle, pull the tail tightly to close the circle.

Insert your hook into the first single crochet stitch you made and make a slip stitch to close the circle.

With your slip stitch complete, you are now ready to start a round.

STARTING A ROUND

To start a round, first begin by using either the chain stitch ring or magic circle method. This example used the magic circle method.

ROUND 1:

Chain 1. Insert your hook under the top 2 loops of the first stitch and work a single crochet into that stitch.

Work 2 single crochets into each of the remaining stitches. (You will have 12 stitches.) Insert your hook back into the first stitch and make a slip stitch to close the round.

ROUNDS 2-6:

Each round increases by 6 stitches. The increases are evenly spaced in order to keep the circular shape. Close each round with a slip stitch back into the first stitch and then chain 1.

Round 2: Single crochet an increase in every other stitch for a total of 18 stitches.

Round 3: Single crochet an increase in every third stitch for a total of 24 stitches.

Round 4: Single crochet an increase in every fourth stitch for a total of 30 stitches.

Round 5: Single crochet an increase in every fifth stitch for a total of 36 stitches.

Round 6: Single crochet an increase in every sixth stitch for a total of 42 stitches.

For additional rounds, continue to evenly increase your rounds by 6 until your desired circumference.

Joining in New Yarn

AT THE END OF A ROW

1

To join in new yarn at the end of a row, work the last stitch with the old yarn until the final yarn over of the stitch. Yarn over with the new yarn.

2

Draw this new yarn through both loops on your hook. There is 1 loop on your hook. Continue stitching with the new yarn as usual.

IN THE MIDDLE OF A ROW

1

To join in new yarn in the middle of a row, work the last stitch with the old yarn until the final yarn over of the stitch. Yarn over with the new yarn.

2

Draw this new yarn through both loops on your hook. There is 1 loop on your hook. Continue stitching with the new yarn as usual until you reach the end of the row.

Tip: Rather than leaving the tail of the old yarn in the middle of the row, you can work over the old yarn until you reach the end of the row. You can then weave in all yarn tails at the edges later.

Fastening Off

After completing your last stitch, cut the excess yarn, leaving several inches to weave the tail in later. Yarn over and draw the yarn tail through the loop on your hook.

Pull the yarn tail to tighten.

Weaving in the Tail

Thread one of your yarn tails into a blunt-tipped tapestry needle. Insert the needle into the first stitch and draw the yarn through.

Continue weaving the needle under and over the stitches around the edge.

Cut the yarn close to the final stitch when you're done weaving in the tail.

Gauge

Gauge refers to how many stitches and rows you should have in a given area in order to match the measurements of a project. The pattern will state how many stitches and rows are needed to achieve the proper gauge. Gauge is most important when making clothing items, like sweaters or socks, in order to get the proper fit.

FOUR THINGS DETERMINE YOUR GAUGE

- Tension (how loosely or tightly you form the stitches)
- Type and weight of the yarn
- Size of thc hook
- Stitch being worked

MAKING YOUR GAUGE SWATCH

Using the same yarn, hook size, and stitch you plan to use for the pattern, crochet a swatch at least 4 x 4 inches. If the project has specific gauge instructions, follow those. After your gauge swatch is complete, lay it on a flat surface.

MEASURING YOUR GAUGE SWATCH

Use a ruler, tape measure, or gauge tool and measure 4 inches across your swatch and mark it with pins. Count the number of stitches between the pins. This is your stitch gauge.

Next you will need to measure the row gauge. Place your measuring tool vertically on the swatch, measure 4 inches, and mark it with pins. Count the number of rows between the pins. This is your row gauge.

ADJUSTING YOUR GAUGE

If your gauge swatch has too many stitches or rows compared to the pattern, use a larger hook. If your gauge swatch doesn't have enough stitches or rows, use a smaller hook. Keep adjusting your hook size until you have the required gauge.

Tip: The stitch gauge is more important than the row gauge. That's because it is easier to adjust the number of rows than to adjust the number of stitches in your crochet project.

Abbreviations & Symbols

Crochet patterns often use abbreviations and symbols as shorthand to represent frequently used stitches and techniques. Use the guide below as you start to follow patterns using shorthand.

Abbreviations

alt	alternate
approx	approximately
beg	begin/beginning
bet	between
BL or blo	back loop or back loop only
bo	bobble
BP	back post
BPdc	back post double crochet
BPhdc	back post half double crochet
BPsc	back post single crochet
BPtr	back post treble crochet
CC	contrasting color
ch	chain(s)
ch-sp	chain space(s)
CL	cluster
cm	centimeter(s)
cont	continue
dc	double crochet(s)
dec	decrease(s)/decreasing
dtr	double treble crochet(s)
FL or flo	front loop or front loop only
FP	front post
FPdc	front post double crochet
FPhdc	front post half double crochet
FPsc	front post single crochet
FPtr	front post treble crochet
hdc	half double crochet(s)
hk	hook
inc	increase(s)/increasing
lp(s)	loop(s)
MC	main color
mm	millimeter(s)
p	picot
pc	popcorn
pat(s)	pattern(s)
pm	place marker
prev	previous
rem	remain/remaining
rep	repeat(s)
rnd(s)	round(s)
RS	right side
sc	single crochet(s)
sl st	slip stitch
sk	skip
sp(s)	space(s)
st(s)	stitch(es)
tch	turning chain(s)
tog	together
tr	treble crochet(s)
WS	wrong side
yd(s)	yard(s)
yo	yarn over
" or in	inch(es)
[ ]	work instructions within brackets as many times as directed
( )	work instructions within parentheses as many times as directed
*****	repeat the instructions following the single asterisk as directed
******	repeat the instructions between asterisks as many times as directed or repeat from a given set of instructions

Symbols

	chain
•	slip stitch
X or +	single crochet
	half double crochet
	double crochet
	treble crochet
	sc2tog
	sc3tog
	dc2tog
	dc3tog
	3-dc cluster
	3-hdc cluster/ puff st/bobble
	5-dc popcorn
	5-dc shell
	ch-3 picot
	front post dc
	back post dc
	worked in back loop only**
	worked in front loop only**

**Symbol appears at base of stitch being worked

Hat Patterns

Easy Hat with Pom-Pom

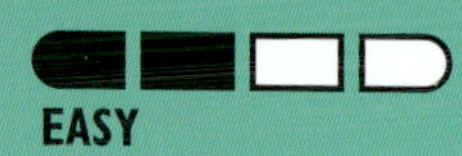

MATERIALS

Yarn: 6 SUPER BULKY 1 skein (106 yd)

We used: Lion Brand Wool-Ease Thick & Quick in Deep Lagoon (80% acrylic, 20% wool; 106 yd [97 m] per 6 oz [170 g] skein)

Hook: 9 mm/U.S. M/N-13

Other: Scissors, tapestry needle

SIZE

23.5" (60 cm) circumference; 8" (20 cm) from top of crown to bottom edge; pom-pom is 4.5" (11.5 cm) high, 10.5" (26.5 cm) circumference

GAUGE

7 sc and 8 rows = 4" (10 cm)

STITCHES USED

Chain stitch (ch)

Double crochet (dc)

Double crochet in back loop only (dc blo)

Single crochet (sc)

Slip stitch (sl st)

INSTRUCTIONS

Hat is worked in rounds. Ch 3, join with sl st to form a ring.

Round 1: Ch 3 (counts as first dc here and throughout), 9 dc in ring (10 dc), sl st to top of beg ch 3.

Round 2: Ch 3, dc in same sp, *2 dc in each next st; repeat from * around (20 dc), sl st to top of beg ch 3.

Round 3: Ch 3, 2 dc in next dc, *dc in next dc, 2 dc in next dc; repeat from * around (30 dc), sl st to top of beg ch 3.

Round 4: Ch 3, dc blo in next st, 2 dc blo in next st, *dc blo in next 2 sts, 2 dc blo in next st; repeat from * around (40 sts), sl st to top of beg ch 3.

Round 5: Ch 3, dc blo in next 2 sts, 2 dc blo in next st, *dc blo in next 3 sts, 2 dc blo in next st; repeat from * around (50 sts), sl st to top of beg ch 3.

Rounds 6–9: Ch 3, dc blo in each next st around (50 sts), sl st to top of beg ch 3.

Fasten off and weave in yarn tails.

How to dc blo: Yo and insert hook under back loop only (rather than under both top loops) of next stitch, then complete the dc as usual: yo and draw through first loop on hook, yo and draw through first 2 loops on hook, yo and draw through remaining 2 loops on hook to complete.

Tip: Using a yarn like this one that adds strands of other colors to the base color is a great choice for anyone who wants subtle color variation without changing yarn during your project. For even more color variety, try using a variegated or self-striping yarn.

Making and attaching a pom-pom

1. Wrap the yarn around your left hand as shown. Hold the yarn tail between your thumb and other fingers, leaving a tail.

2. Wrap the working yarn around your left hand in the same area to keep width uniform. You can also wrap yarn around a book, piece of foam board, or many other items instead of your hand.

3. Stop wrapping when satisfied with the fullness. The more wraps, the fuller the pom-pom. For this example, about 60 wraps.

4. Remove yarn wraps from your left hand. The wraps will form a large loop.

5. Wrap the working yarn (the longer yarn tail) twice around the middle of the large loop.

6. Tie the working yarn tail in a knot with the shorter yarn tail from step 1. Do not cut the longer working yarn tail; you will use this later to attach pom-pom to hat.

7. Use scissors to cut the closed loops on one side of the center tie.

8. Cut the closed loops on the other side of center tie. Cut any remaining closed loops to release the pom-pom.

9. Trim any extra-long ends (but not the working yarn tail), shaping into a smooth, uniform ball.

Making and attaching a pom-pom (continued)

10. When you're satisfied with shape of pom-pom, thread a tapestry needle with the yarn tail.

11. With hat right side out, insert the needle in top of hat under a stitch.

12. Continue weaving needle under each stitch around. Do extra stitches into the pom-pom, then into the hat, three times to secure.

13. Turn hat inside out (wrong side out). Tie knot on inside of hat. Weave under any stitches on inside of hat.

14. Turn hat right side out to complete.

Using a pom-pom maker: Open up both arms of pom-pom maker. Wrap yarn around one arm desired number of times. Bring yarn across top of center wheel, then wrap around 2nd arm same number of times. Close arms of pom-pom maker. Cut excess yarn. Put scissors into groove and cut through center of one wrapped arm; repeat for 2nd wrapped arm. Cut 12" length of matching yarn. Wrap yarn around pom-pom maker, along groove where you cut. Tie 2 really tight knots on one side. Wrap yarn around to other side and tie 2 really tight knots there. Open up arms and pull halves apart to release pom-pom. Leave 2 long ends to attach pom-pom to hat.

Twisted Ear Warmer

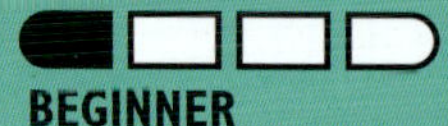

MATERIALS

Yarn: 

less than 194 yards

We used: Patons Classic Wool Worsted in Pink Quartz (100% wool; 194 yd [177 m] per 3.5 oz [100 g] ball)

Hook: 5.5 mm/U.S. I-9

Other: Scissors, tape measure, tapestry needle

SIZE

18" (46 cm) circumference when joined;
4.25" (11 cm) wide

GAUGE

13 sc and 16 rows = 4" (10 cm)

STITCHES USED

Chain stitch (ch)

Double crochet (dc)

Single crochet (sc)

Whipstitch

INSTRUCTIONS

Ear warmer is worked in rows. Ch 17.

Row 1: Sc in 2nd ch from hook and in each ch to end of row, turn.

Row 2: Ch 3, sc in next st, *dc in next st, sc in next st; repeat from * to end of row, turn.

Repeat row 2 until piece measures about 20".

Fasten off, leaving a long 12" tail for joining.

Joining with a twist

Tip: You can use the same technique to make a twisted ear warmer with a piece of crocheted fabric (as demonstrated here), a piece of knitted fabric, or any piece of fabric—it works the same regardless.

1. Lay the piece flat with right side facing up. Fold both short edges in on themselves, pinching each side as shown.

2. Fit the folds together to make a tight sandwich with 4 layers of fabric.

3. Thread a tapestry needle with long yarn tail or new matching yarn.

4. Whipstitch through all 4 layers along seam as follows: insert needle from front to back through first set of stitches and draw yarn through. Bring needle over the top and insert from front to back through next set of stitches to the left, drawing yarn through.

5. Repeat step 4 across the seam, making sure your whipstitches go through all 4 layers.

6. Turn ear warmer. Whipstitch across same seam again, this time inserting needle from back to front through each set of stitches and drawing yarn through. Bring needle up over the top and insert from back to front through next set of stitches to the left.

7. Turn ear warmer right side out. Weave in yarn tails.

Tip: This pattern does not use the full 194-yard ball, so you will have plenty of leftover yarn for use in another project.

Serene Stripes Beanie

MATERIALS

Yarn:  in 3 colors, less than 360 yards of each color

We used: Bernat Premium in Sky Gray, Baby Blue, and Sky Blue (100% acrylic; 360 yd [329 m] per 7 oz [198 g] ball)

Hook: 5.5 mm/U.S. I-9

Other: Scissors, tapestry needle

SIZE

22" (56 cm) circumference; 7.5" (19 cm) from top to bottom edge

GAUGE

12 sc and 12 rows = 4" (10 cm)

STITCHES USED

Chain stitch (ch)
Half double crochet (hdc)
Single crochet (sc)
Slip stitch (sl st)

Tip: Color A = Sky Gray; color B = Baby Blue; color C = Sky Blue. This pattern requires far less than 360 yards of each color; you'll have plenty of leftover yarn to use for other projects.

INSTRUCTIONS

With color A (here in Sky Gray), ch 3, sl st in first ch made to form a ring.

Round 1: Ch 2 (counts as first hdc here and throughout), 11 hdc in ring. (12 sts)

Round 2: Ch 2, hdc in same st, *2 hdc in next st; repeat from * around, sl st to top of beg ch 2. (24 sts)

Round 3: Ch 2, 2 hdc in next st, *hdc in next st, 2 hdc in next st; repeat from * around, sl st to top of beg ch 2. (36 sts)

Round 4: Ch 2, hdc in next st, 2 hdc in next st, *hdc in next 2 sts, 2 hdc in next st; repeat from * around, sl st to top of beg ch 2. (48 sts)

Round 5: Ch 2, hdc in next 2 sts, 2 hdc in next st, *hdc in next 3 sts, 2 hdc in next st; repeat from * around, sl st to top of beg ch 2. (60 sts)

Round 6: Attach color B (Baby Blue) on top of ch 2 in previous round, ch 2, hdc in next 3 sts, 2 hdc in next st, *hdc in next 4 sts, 2 hdc in next st; repeat from * around, sl st to top of beg ch 2. (72 sts)

Round 7: Ch 2, hdc in next 12 sts, 2 hdc in next st, *hdc in next 13 sts, 2 hdc in next st; repeat from * around, sl st to top of beg ch 2. (76 sts)

Round 8: Ch 2, hdc in each st around, sl st to top of beg ch 2. (76 sts)

Rounds 9–11: Attach color C (Sky Blue) on top of ch 2 in previous round. Repeat round 8.

Rounds 12–14: Attach color A (Sky Gray) on top of ch 2 in previous round. Repeat round 8.

Rounds 15–17: Attach color B (Baby Blue) on top of ch 2 in previous round. Repeat round 8.

Rounds 18–20: Attach color C (Sky Blue) on top of ch 2 in previous round. Repeat round 8.

Round 21: Ch 1, sc in each st around, sl st in ch-1 sp.

Fasten off and weave in all yarn tails.

Spiral Cap with Brim

MATERIALS

Yarn: (4 MEDIUM) less than 315 yards

We used: Caron Simply Soft in Dark Sage (100% acrylic; 315 yd [288 m] per 6 oz [170 g] ball)

Hook: 5.5 mm/U.S. I-9

Other: 2 buttons, tapestry needle

SIZE

21" (53 cm) circumference; 7.5" (19 cm) from top of crown to brim on side of hat; brim is 2.5" (5 cm) wide at widest point

GAUGE

12 sc and 12 rows = 4" (10 cm)

STITCHES USED

Chain stitch (ch)

Double crochet (dc)

Front post double crochet (FPdc)

Half double crochet (hdc)

Single crochet (sc)

Slip stitch (sl st)

INSTRUCTIONS

Hat is worked in rounds, then the brim is worked in rows.

Ch 3, sl st in 3rd ch from hook to form a ring.

Round 1: Ch 3 (counts as first dc here and throughout), 9 dc in ring (10 dc), sl st to top of beg ch 3.

Round 2: Ch 3, dc in same st, 2 dc in each st around (20 dc), sl st to top of beg ch 3.

Round 3: Ch 3, FPdc in same st, *dc in next st, FPdc in same st; repeat from * around. (40 sts)

Round 4: Repeat round 3.

Round 5: Ch 3, *FPdc in next FPdc, 2 dc in sp between FPdc and next dc; repeat from * around until last FPdc, FPdc in last FPdc, dc in sp between FPdc and beg ch 3, sl st to top of beg ch 3.

Round 6: Repeat round 5.

Round 7: Ch 3, *FPdc in next FPdc, 3 dc in sp between FPdc and next dc; repeat from * around until last FPdc, FPdc in last FPdc, 2 dc in sp between FPdc and beg ch 3, sl st to top of beg ch 3.

Rounds 8–17: Repeat round 7.

Rounds 18–19: Ch 1, sc in each st around, sl st to first sc.

How to FPdc: Yarn over and insert hook under post of next stitch from the front side, yarn over and draw yarn around post, yarn over and draw yarn through first 2 loops on hook, yarn over and draw yarn through remaining 2 loops on hook to complete the FPdc.

Shape brim

Begin working in rows to shape the brim.

Row 1: Ch 1, sc in next 50 sts, turn.

Row 2: Ch 2, hdc in each st around, turn.

Rows 3–6: Repeat row 2.

Fasten off.

Finishing

Fold brim of hat up at both corners up and sew into place with a button on each side. Weave in all yarn tails when done.

Flower Cloche

MATERIALS

Yarn: 

in 2 colors, 1 skein (106 yards) of each color

We used: Lion Brand Wool-Ease Thick & Quick in Driftwood and Raspberry (80% acrylic, 20% wool; 106 yd [97 m] per 6 oz [170 g] skein)

Hook: 9 mm/U.S. M/N-13

Other: Tapestry needle

SIZE

23" (58.5 cm) circumference; 8" (20 cm) from top of crown to bottom edge

GAUGE

7 sc and 8 rows = 4" (10 cm)

STITCHES USED

Chain stitch (ch)

Double crochet (dc)

Double crochet in back loop only (dc blo)

Half double crochet in back loop only (hdc blo)

Single crochet (sc)

Single crochet in back loop only (sc blo)

Slip stitch (sl st)

INSTRUCTIONS

Hat is worked in rounds from the top down.

With main color (here in Driftwood), ch 3, join with sl st to form a ring.

Tip: Main color is Driftwood; contrast color is Raspberry. You won't need a full 106-yard skein of the contrast color.

Round 1: Ch 3 (counts as first dc here and throughout), 11 dc in ring (12 dc), sl st to top of beg ch 3.

Round 2: Ch 3, dc in same st, 2 dc in each st around (24 dc), sl st to top of beg ch 3.

Round 3: Ch 3, *2 dc in next dc, 1 dc in next dc; repeat from * around (36 dc), sl st to top of beg ch 3.

Round 4: Ch 3, dc in next st, 2 dc in next st, *dc in next 2 sts, 2 dc in next st; repeat from * around (48 dc), sl st to top of beg ch 3.

Round 5: Ch 1, sc blo in each dc around (48 sc), sl st in first sc.

Round 6: Ch 3, dc blo in each sc around (48 dc), sl st to top of beg ch 3.

Rounds 7–8: Repeat rounds 5–6. Do not fasten off with color A; instead drop it.

How to sc blo: Insert hook under back loop only (rather than under both top loops) of next stitch, then complete the sc as usual: yo and draw yarn through first loop on hook, yo and draw yarn through both loops on hook to complete.

Attach contrast color (here in Raspberry) on top of ch 3 in round 8.

Round 9: With contrast color (Raspberry), ch 2, hdc blo in each st around (48 hdc), sl st to top of beg ch 2. Fasten off.

How to hdc blo: Yo and insert hook under back loop only of next stitch, then complete the hdc as usual: yo and draw through first loop on hook, yo and draw through all 3 loops on hook to complete.

Round 10: Pick up main color (Driftwood) and ch 3. Repeat round 6.

Round 11: Repeat round 5.

Fasten off and weave in yarn tails.

Flower

With contrast color (Raspberry), ch 3, join with sl st to form a ring.

Round 1: Work [ch 6, sc in ring] 6 times.

Round 2: Work [ch 8, sc in ring between next 2 sc] 6 times.

Fasten off, leaving a 12" tail for sewing.

Finishing

Sew the flower onto the hat and weave in all yarn tails.

How to dc blo: Yo and insert hook under back loop only of next stitch, then complete the dc as usual: yo and draw through first loop on hook, yo and draw through first 2 loops on hook, yo and draw through remaining 2 loops on hook to complete.

Messy Hair Hat

MATERIALS

Yarn: 4 MEDIUM in 3 colors, less than 194 yards of each color

We used: Patons Classic Wool Worsted in Winter White, Rich Grass, and Navy Blue (100% wool; 194 yd [177 m] per 3.5 oz [100 g] ball)

Hook: 5.5 mm/U.S. I-9

Other: Tapestry needle

SIZE

22" (56 cm) circumference; 7.75" (19.5 cm) from top to bottom edge; opening is about 2" (5 cm) across

GAUGE

13 sc and 15 rows = 4" (10 cm)

STITCHES USED

Chain stitch (ch)

Cluster (CL)

Double crochet (dc)

Single crochet (sc)

Slip stitch (sl st)

V-stitch

INSTRUCTIONS

Tip: Color A = Winter White; color B = Rich Grass; color C = Navy Blue.

With color A (here in Winter White), ch 20, sl st in first ch made to form a ring.

Round 1: Ch 3, 23 dc in ring, sl st to top of beg ch 3.

Round 2: Ch 3, CL in same st, *dc in next dc, CL in next dc; rep from * around, sl st to top of beg ch 3.

Round 3: Ch 3, CL in same st, *dc in next dc, CL in next CL; rep from * around, sl st to top of beg ch 3. Fasten off color A.

Round 4: Attach color B (Rich Grass) in any dc, ch 4, dc in same dc where you attached yarn, *CL in next CL, v-stitch in next dc; rep from * around, sl st on 3rd ch of beg ch 4 you did after attaching yarn.

Rounds 5–7: Sl st into next v-stitch, ch 4, dc in same st, *CL in next CL, v-stitch in next v-stitch; rep from * around, sl st on 3rd ch of beg ch 4. Fasten off color B.

Round 8: Attach color A (Winter White) in any v-stitch. Repeat above instructions for rounds 5–7 once, creating just one new round. Fasten off color A.

Round 9: Attach color B (Rich Grass) in any v-stitch, ch 4, dc in same st, *CL in next CL, v-stitch in next v-stitch; rep from * around, sl st on 3rd ch of beg ch 4. Fasten off color B.

Round 10: Attach color C (Navy Blue) in any v-stitch, ch 4, dc in same st, *CL in next CL, v-stitch in next v-stitch; rep from * around, sl st on 3rd ch of beg ch 4.

Rounds 11–12: Ch 4, dc in same st, *CL in next CL, v-stitch in next v-stitch; rep from * around, sl st on 3rd ch of beg ch 4.

Rounds 13–15: Ch 1, sc in each st around, sl st to beg ch 1.

Fasten off and weave in all yarn tails.

How to make the v-stitch: Work [dc, ch 1, dc] in one stitch.

How to make the cluster: Yo and insert hook into indicated st or sp, yo and draw through first loop on hook, [yo and draw through first 2 loops on hook] 3 times, yo and draw through all remaining loops on hook to complete.

Shell Stitch Hat with Pom-Pom

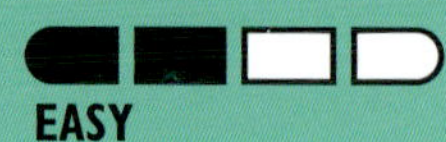

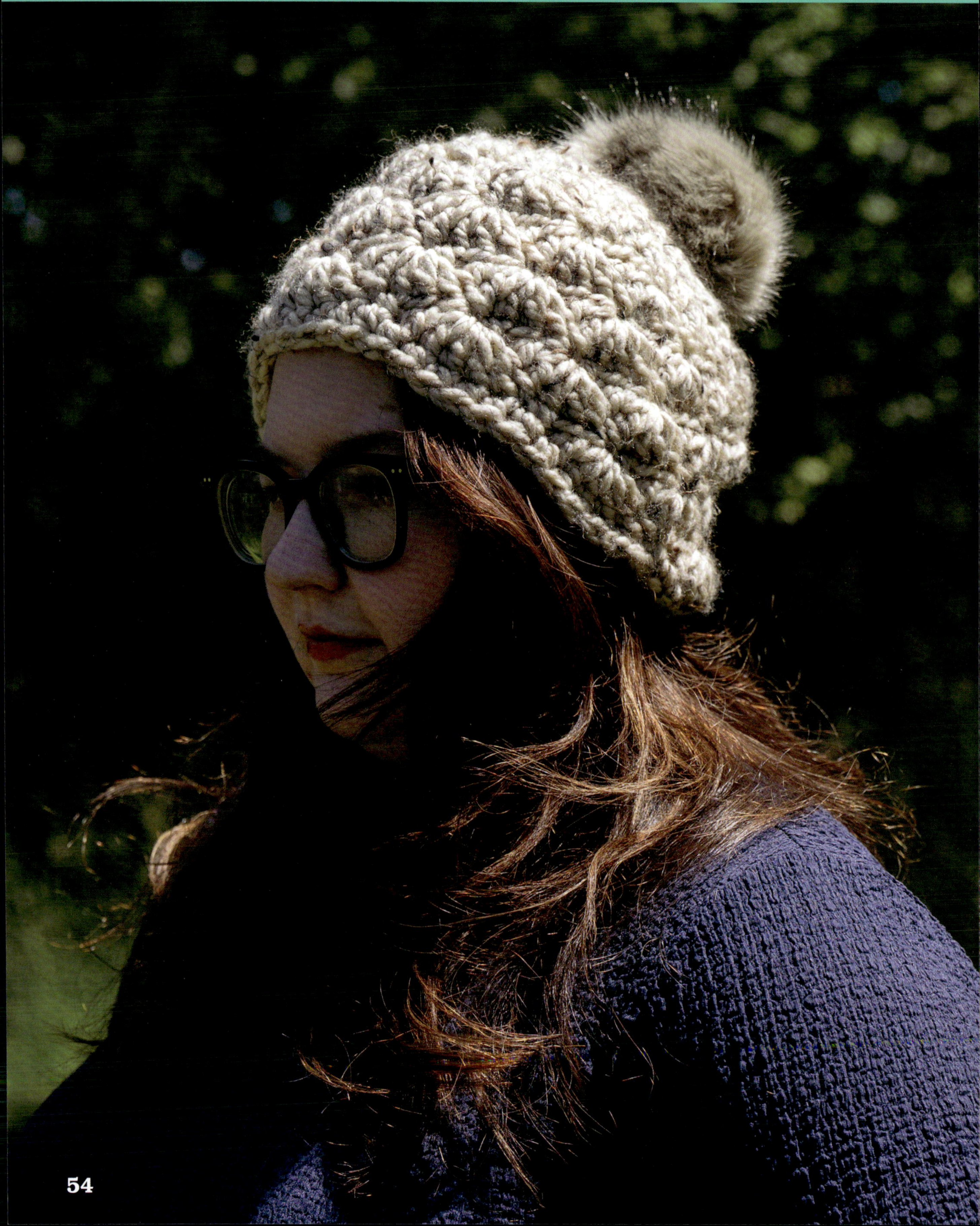

MATERIALS

Yarn: 6 SUPER BULKY 1 skein (106 yards)

We used: Lion Brand Wool-Ease Thick & Quick in Oatmeal (82% acrylic, 10% wool, 8% rayon; 106 yd [97 m] per 6 oz [170 g] skein)

Hook: 9 mm/U.S. M/N-13

Other: Bernat Faux Fur Pom-Pom in Gray Lynx (85% acrylic, 15% polyester), sewing needle, tapestry needle

SIZE

Nearly 24" (61 cm) circumference; 8.5" (21.5 cm) from top to bottom edge; pom-pom is about 4" (10 cm) high, 10.5" (26.5 cm) circumference

GAUGE

7 sc and 8 rows = 4" (10 cm)

STITCHES USED

Chain stitch (ch)

Double crochet (dc)

Half double crochet (hdc)

Shell stitch

Single crochet (sc)

Slip stitch (sl st)

INSTRUCTIONS

Ch 3, sl st in 3rd ch from hook to form a ring.

Round 1: Ch 3 (counts as first dc here and throughout), 11 dc in ring (12 dc), sl st to top of beg ch 3.

Round 2: Ch 3, dc in same st, 2 dc in each st around (24 dc), sl st to top of beg ch 3.

Round 3: Ch 3, *2 dc in next dc, 1 dc in next dc; repeat from * around (36 dc), end with 2 dc in next st, sl st to top of beg ch 3.

Round 4: Ch 3, dc in next st, 2 dc in next st, *dc in next 2 sts, 2 dc in next st; repeat from * around (48 dc), sl st to top of beg ch 3.

Round 5: Ch 3, 2 dc in same st, *skip 2 sts, shell st in next st, skip 2 sts, sc in next st; repeat from * 6 more times, 2 dc in last st, sl st to top of beg ch 3.

Rounds 6–9: Repeat round 5.

Round 10: Ch 1, sc in each dc and hdc in each sc around, sl st in beg ch 1.

Fasten off.

How to make the shell stitch: Work 5 dc in the same stitch where indicated.

Attaching the faux fur pom-pom

1. Thread one of the strings onto a sharper-than-usual tapestry needle or sewing needle.

2. With the right side of the hat facing out, sew under and over about halfway around the top.

3. Insert the needle into the hat, then into the core of the pom-pom. Repeat twice more.

4. Insert the needle into the inside (wrong side) of the hat and draw through. Remove needle from string.

5. Thread the other string onto the needle. Repeat steps 2–4.

6. Turn the hat inside out to better access the 2 strings.

7. Tie the strings in a tight knot twice for 2 knots total.

8. Thread both strings through the eye of the needle. Weave across top of hat.

9. Take the 2 strings in one hand and the leftover yarn tail in the other hand.

10. Tie a knot with the strings and yarn tail. Weave in or trim ends when done.

Tip: Faux fur pom-poms come with various attachment mechanisms. Some come with snaps or elastic loops. This one comes with 2 strings to attach the pom-pom to the hat.

Bright Stripes Beanie

MATERIALS

Yarn:  in 5 colors, less than 360 yards of each color

We used: Bernat Premium in White, Green, Grand Purple, Coral Peach, and Baby Yellow (100% acrylic; 360 yd [329 m] per 7 oz [198 g] ball)

Hook: 5.5 mm/U.S. I-9

Other: Tapestry needle

SIZE

22" (56 cm) circumference; 8.25" (21 cm) from top of crown to bottom edge

GAUGE

12 sc and 12 rows = 4" (10 cm)

STITCHES USED

Back post double crochet (BPdc)

Chain stitch (ch)

Double crochet (dc)

Front post double crochet (FPdc)

Magic circle

Single crochet (sc)

Slip stitch (sl st)

INSTRUCTIONS

Hat is worked in rounds from the top down.

With color A (here in White), make a magic circle.

Round 1: Ch 3, 2 dc in circle, *ch 1, 3 dc in circle; rep from * 2 more times, ch 1, sl st to top of beg ch 3. Fasten off color A.

Round 2: Attach color B (Green) in any ch-1 sp, (ch 3, 2 dc, ch 2, 3 dc) in the same sp, *(3 dc, ch 2, 3 dc) in next ch-1 sp; repeat from * 2 more times, sl st to top of beg ch 3. Fasten off color B.

Round 3: Attach color C (Grand Purple) in any ch-2 sp, (ch 3, 2 dc, ch 2, 3 dc) in the same ch-2 sp where you attached yarn, skip next 3 dc, 3 dc in next sp, *(3 dc, ch 2, 3 dc) in next ch-2 sp, skip next 3 dc, 3 dc in next sp; repeat from * 2 more times, sl st to top of beg ch 3. Fasten off color C.

Round 4: Attach color D (Coral Peach) in any ch-2 sp, ch 3, 2 dc in the same ch-2 sp where you attached yarn, skip next 3 dc, 3 dc in next sp, skip next 3 dc, (3 dc, ch 2, 3 dc) in next sp. *Skip next 3 dc, 3 dc in next sp twice, skip next 3 dc, (3 dc, ch 2, 3 dc) in next sp; repeat from * 2 more times, sl st to top of beg ch 3. Fasten off color D.

Round 5: Attach color E (Baby Yellow) in any ch-2 sp, (ch 3, 2 dc, 3 dc) in the same sp, (skip next 3 dc, 3 dc in next sp) 3 times, *(3 dc, ch 2, 3 dc) in next sp, (skip next 3 dc, 3 dc in next sp) 3 times; repeat from * 2 more times, sl st to top of beg ch 3. Fasten off color E.

Round 6: Attach color A (White) in any sp between 3 dc, (ch 3, 2 dc) in the same sp, *skip next 3 dc, 3 dc in next sp; repeat from * to the last sp, sl st to top of beg ch 3. Fasten off.

Round 7: With color B (Green), repeat round 6.

Round 8: With color C (Grand Purple), repeat round 6.

Round 9: With color D (Coral Peach), repeat round 6.

Round 10: With color E (Baby Yellow), repeat round 6.

Rounds 11–15: Repeat rounds 6–10.

Tip: Color A = White; color B = Green; color C = Grand Purple; color D = Coral Peach; color E = Baby Yellow. You'll need far less than the 360 yards of each ball to complete the hat.

Ribbing

Round 1: Attach color A (White) on top of ch 3 in previous round, ch 3, *FPdc in next dc, BPdc in next dc; repeat from * around. Sl st to top of beg ch 3.

Round 2: Ch 3, *FPdc in the front post st, BPdc in the back post st; repeat from * around. Sl st to top of beg ch 3.

Round 3: Repeat round 2.

Fasten off and weave in all yarn tails.

How to BPdc: Yarn over and insert hook under post of next stitch from the back side (the post of the stitch is behind your hook). Yarn over and draw yarn around post. Yarn over and draw yarn through first 2 loops on hook. Yarn over and draw through remaining 2 loops on hook to complete the BPdc.

How to FPdc: Yarn over and insert hook under post of next stitch from the front side (the post of the stitch is in front of your hook). Yarn over and draw yarn around post. Yarn over and draw yarn through first 2 loops on hook. Yarn over and draw yarn through remaining 2 loops on hook to complete the FPdc.

Slouchy Beret

MATERIALS

Yarn:  less than 315 yards

We used: Caron Simply Soft in Burgundy (100% acrylic; 315 yd [288 m] per 6 oz [170 g] ball)

Hook: 5.5 mm/U.S. I-9

Other: Tapestry needle

SIZE

19" (48 cm) circumference; 7.5" (19 cm) from top of crown to bottom edge

GAUGE

14 dc and 8 rows = 4" (10 cm)

STITCHES USED

Chain stitch (ch)

Double crochet (dc)

Double crochet 2 together (dc2tog)

Puff stitch

Single crochet (sc)

Slip stitch (sl st)

INSTRUCTIONS

Ch 4, sl st in 4th ch from hook to form a ring.

Round 1: 8 puff sts in the ring, sl st on top of first puff st, sl st in next sp between first and 2nd puff sts.

Round 2: Ch 3, puff st, ch 1, puff st in the same sp, *(puff st, ch 1, puff st) in next sp between 2 puff sts in prev rnd; rep from * 6 more times, sl st to top of beg ch 3.

Round 3: Ch 3, *(puff st, ch 1, puff st) in next ch-1 sp between 2 puff sts in prev rnd, dc in next sp; rep from * 6 more times, (puff st, ch 1, puff st) in last ch-1 sp, sl st to top of beg ch 3.

Round 4: Ch 3, *(puff st, ch 1, puff st) in next ch-1 sp between 2 puff sts in prev rnd, dc in next sp twice; rep from * 6 more times, (puff st, ch 1, puff st) in last ch-1 sp, dc in next sp, sl st to top of beg ch 3.

Round 5: Ch 3, *(puff st, ch 1, puff st) in next ch-1 sp between 2 puff sts in prev rnd, dc in next sp 3 times; rep from * 6 more times, (puff st, ch 1, puff st) in last ch-1 sp, dc in next sp twice, sl st to top of beg ch 3.

Round 6: Ch 3, *(puff st, ch 1, puff st) in next ch-1 sp between 2 puff sts in prev rnd, dc in next sp 4 times; rep from * 6 more times, (puff st, ch 1, puff st) in last ch-1 sp, dc in next sp 3 times, sl st to top of beg ch 3.

Round 7: Ch 3, *(puff st, ch 1, puff st) in next ch-1 sp between 2 puff sts in prev rnd, dc in next sp 5 times; rep from * 6 more times, (puff st, ch 1, puff st) in last ch-1 sp, dc in next sp 4 times, sl st to top of beg ch 3.

Round 8: Ch 3, *(puff st, ch 1, puff st) in next ch-1 sp between 2 puff sts in prev rnd, dc in next sp 6 times; rep from * 6 more times, (puff st, ch 1, puff st) in last ch-1 sp, dc in next sp 5 times, sl st to top of beg ch 3.

How to make the puff stitch: Yo and insert hk in specified st/sp, [yo and draw through, pulling up a long lp] 3 times, yo and draw through all 7 lps on hk, ch 1 to close and secure the puff st.

Round 9: Ch 3, *(puff st, ch 1, puff st) in next ch-1 sp between 2 puff sts in prev rnd, dc in next sp 7 times; rep from * 6 more times, (puff st, ch 1, puff st) in last ch-1 sp, dc in next sp 6 times, sl st to top of beg ch 3.

Rounds 10–14: Repeat round 9.

Round 15: Ch 3, *(puff st, ch 1, puff st) in next ch-1 sp between 2 puff sts in prev rnd, dc2tog in next 2 sps, dc in next sp 3 times, dc2tog in next 2 sps; rep from * 6 more times, (puff st, ch 1, puff st) in last ch-1 sp of rnd, dc2tog in next 2 sps, dc in next sp 3 times, dc in next sp, sl st to top of beg ch 3.

Round 16: Repeat round 15.

Rounds 17–20: Ch 1, sc in each st around.

Fasten off and weave in yarn tails.

How to dc2tog: Yo and insert hk in next st, yo and draw through st (3 lps on hk), yo and draw through first 2 lps on hk (2 lps left on hk), yo and insert hk in next st, yo and draw through st (4 lps on hk), yo and draw through first 2 lps on hk (3 lps on hk), yo and draw through all 3 lps on hk.

Ribbed Hat

MATERIALS

Yarn: 

299 yards total

We used: 2 skeins Lion Brand Wool-Ease in Gray Heather (80% acrylic, 20% wool; 197 yd [180 m] per 3 oz [85 g] skein)

Hook: 6 mm/U.S. J-10

Other: Scissors, tape measure, tapestry needle

SIZE

23" (58.5 cm) circumference; 10.75" (27 cm) from top of crown to bottom edge uncuffed, 8" (20 cm) to bottom edge cuffed; pom-pom is 2.5" (6 cm) high, 10" (25.5 cm) circumference

GAUGE

15 hdc and 12 rows = 4" (10 cm)

STITCHES USED

Chain stitch (ch)
Front 2 loops half double crochet (f2lhdc)
Half double crochet (hdc)

INSTRUCTIONS

Hat is worked from side to side in rows, joined to form a tube, then cinched close at the top.

Ch 41.

Row 1: Hdc in 3rd ch from hook, *hdc in next ch; rep from * to end of row. Ch 2, turn. (40 sts)

Row 2: *F2lhdc in next hdc; rep from * to end of row. Ch 2, turn.

Repeat row 2 until piece measures about 40". Fasten off, leaving a 30" tail for sewing.

How to make the f2lhdc

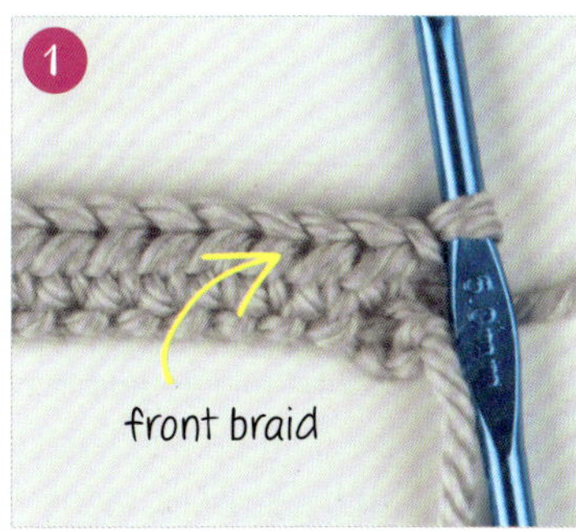

1. At the start of row 2, you'll notice there are 2 braids or sets of Vs running horizontally: one running across the top of your work (consisting of the top 2 loops where you ordinarily work stitches), and another across the front of your work. Both braids include the top loop closer to you.

2. Yarn over. Insert your hook up and under the front 2 loops (rather than under the top 2 loops) of the next stitch, working into the front braid rather than the top braid.

3. Yarn over. Draw yarn through those front 2 loops. You will have 3 loops on your hook.

4. Complete the hdc as usual: yarn over and draw through all 3 loops. You will have 1 loop on your hook when the f2lhdc is complete.

Finishing

Thread the 30" tail through a tapestry needle. Sew the left and right ends together to form a tube with the ridges vertical. Once your tube is formed, follow the steps below to close the hat.

Closing the hat

1. With right side facing out and using a tail about 24" long leftover from joining rectangle into a tube, thread tapestry needle.

2. Weave the threaded needle under ridges along the top of tube.

3. Pull every several stitches to begin closing top of hat like a drawstring.

4. Repeat steps 2–3 around top of tube, pulling as tight as possible once reaching point where stitches began to close hole. The pulling will become more difficult and awkward as you go.

5. Pass needle to the inside (wrong side) of hat. Turn hat inside out.

6. Continue stitching around on the inside, going into every second or third bump to close the hat more securely.

7. Fasten off and weave in yarn tails.

8. Turn hat right side out again.

Pom-pom

Using the pom-pom instructions on pages 42–43 as a guide, wrap yarn around your hand approximately 100 times. Tie tightly in the middle and leave a long 12" tail for attaching the pom-pom to hat. Cut all loops and trim pom-pom into a smooth, round shape. Using a tapestry needle and the 12" tail, sew securely to top of hat.